Right@Sight
Grade 3

Based on
Read and Play
(original and new series) by
T. A. Johnson

Revised by Caroline Evans

With additional material by Paul Terry

EDITION PETERS

London · Frankfurt · Leipzig · New York

Peters Edition Limited
10–12 Baches Street
London
N1 6DN

First published 2001
© 2001 by Hinrichsen Edition, Peters Edition Limited, London

Music-setting and typesetting by Musonix

Cover design by Nick Wakelin and Adam Hay
Text design by c eye, London
Printed in Great Britain by Caligraving Limited
Thetford, Norfolk

Set in Monotype Garamond 3 and Frutiger

Right@Sight

Grade 3

A note to teachers

Sight-reading is one of the most important skills for any musician, and certainly not to be seen as a chore necessary only for passing exams! Right@Sight will help to develop and improve that skill, providing a structured approach and opportunities for regular practice. Hints are provided for the earlier pieces to focus attention on notation, form, interpretation and technique, prompted with questions (left-hand column) and information (right). Suggestions to sight-sing phrases are included to promote aural awareness while playing.

In an examination, half a minute will be given to prepare the sight-reading, and the examiner is likely to remind candidates that they may play the music during this time. Encourage your students to try out the opening, the ending and any awkward-looking passages so that they are well prepared before the test starts. Instil careful attention to the fundamental elements of Time, Rhythm and Key – though the key signature comes first on the staff, it is often the first piece of information to be forgotten in performance!

Becoming a good sight-reader needs daily practice, and regular 'exercise' with Right@Sight will prepare students to tackle whatever music they may want to play. Towards the end of the section with commentary, some pieces go a little beyond the standard expected for the grade, so as to stretch players' ability and enable them to face any sight-reading test with increased confidence: to play it right – at sight!

Caroline Evans

Key to symbols

1	Exercise number
T	Time
R	Rhythm
K	Key
?	Questions
!	Watch out

Contents

Focusing on the keys of C, G, D, A and F major; A, D and E Minor

1

| **T** | What is the time signature? | The value of each beat is a crotchet. |

R Can you tap the rhythm: right hand on the right knee and left hand on the left knee?

Count while tapping.

K What is the key?

Play the tonic (key-note).

? On which beat does the right hand begin?

Observe the rests, particularly those in bar 6.

Are there any broken chords?

Notice the broken octaves in bars 4 and 7 (LH).

Can you look carefully at the fingering, especially in bar 7 (RH)?

There is also a change of hand position at bar 7 (RH).

Play the piece fairly fast (*Allegretto*). Try not to look at the keyboard. Look ahead.

2 Follow the **TRaK**

? What is the time signature?

Count three *quaver* beats per bar in this piece.

! **Watch out** for the accidentals in bars 6 and 7 (LH).

Play this piece steadily. Be sure to count all three quaver beats in bar 4.

Follow the [TRaK]

[?] Are there any accidentals?

Can you study the fingering?

[!] **Watch out** for the intervals in bars 3 and 4, both hands.

Play the tonic chord. Find all the F♯s.

Notice how the C♯ in bar 4 suggests a change of key. Name the new key.

Practise moving to the changes of hand position in bars 4 and 8 (RH) before playing.

Play through very lightly and gracefully, observing the slurs and *staccato* notes on the way.

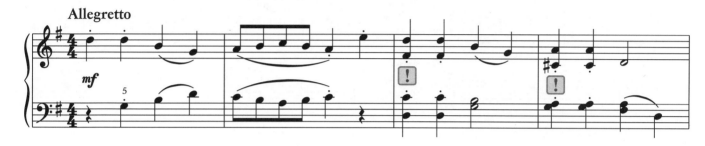

[TRaK]

[?] On which beat does the melody begin?

Are there any accidentals?

Can you study the suggested fingering?

Count three crotchet beats before you play.

There is a suggestion of another key in bar 6. Try to name it.

Be prepared for the changes of hand position in bar 2 (RH) and bar 4.

[TRaK]

[?] Why not try playing the intervals of a fifth
in bar 4, both hands, before you begin?

[!] **Watch out** for the semibreve in bar 7 which should be held while playing the crotchets above.

Find all the F♯s.
Observe the rests in bars 2, 3, and 5.

Name and play the interval on the first
beat in bar 8 (LH).

Observe the phrasing. Play very lightly, but remember the accented G in bar 3 (RH).

[!]

[TRaK]

[?] When you compare the two phrases, which
hand has the melody?

If you are not sure of the key, look for any accidentals,
and then play the tonic in the last bar. Find all the B♭s.

Observe all the rests.

Notice also how the left hand appears to imitate the
right hand in bars 2 and 3.

Observe the *staccato* notes and play this piece lightly and fairly fast (*Allegretto*).

T	How many beats are there in a bar?	Give the value of the beat.
R	Can you clap the rhythm accurately?	The timing of the ♩. ♪ rhythm needs care.
K	What is the key?	Find all the F♯s and any accidentals.
?	Is there any imitation between treble and bass?	Also look for any contrary motion between the hands.

Do not confuse the dotted crotchets with *staccato* notes. Keep counting steadily as you play this piece through.

TRaK		Find the F♯s and any accidentals.
?	Can you observe all the rests?	Play the ledger line notes in bars 1 and 2 (LH) before you begin.
	Can you find the many intervals of a third?	Make sure that when you play the chords, both notes are sounded at the same time, especially in bar 4 (RH).

Put in your own expression marks. Pause 𝄐 slightly in bar 6 and prepare for the chords in bars 7 and 8.
Contrast the slurs with the *staccato* notes. Play gracefully and confidently.

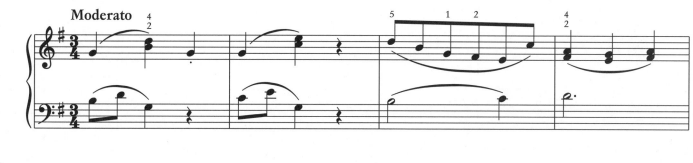

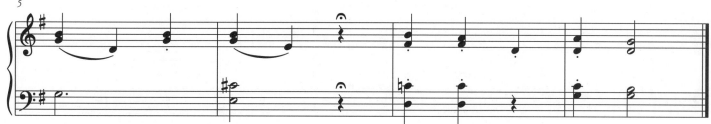

T On which beat does the left hand begin?

R Can you tap the rhythm, both parts together?   Hold all the minims for their full value.

K What does the key signature tell you?   Find **all** the notes to be sharpened.

? Are there any tied notes?   Do not confuse ties with slurs.

Can you look carefully at the fingering?   Play the chords in the last three bars with correct fingering before you begin the piece.

Try and hear the melody in your head before you play this through firmly in a marching style.

T How many beats are there in a bar?

R   Tap the dotted rhythm in bars 1, 3, 5 and 8.

K Is the key major or minor?   Notice the use of D♯ and look at the tonic (bar 10, RH).

? Are there any tied notes?   Try out the chords in bars 7 and 8 before you begin.

Play very *legato* and try to make vivid contrasts in the dynamics. The chords in bar 9 (RH) also need care.

T

Time the semiquavers accurately, four semiquavers to one crotchet beat.

R Can you tap semiquavers with your right hand while your left hand taps crotchets?

Tap this rhythm a number of times:

K Can you find all the notes affected by the key signature?

Move your hand into the keys a little to avoid awkward stretches for the fingers when you play the black notes.

T What does the time signature tell you?

R Can you count as you tap the rhythm?

Left hand entries must be precise in bars 1 and 3.

K Can you name the key?

Find any notes affected by the key signature.

? Can you study the fingering, especially bars 5 and 6 (RH)?

Note the contraction (closing in) between 4th finger and thumb in bar 2 (RH) in order to prepare the 3rd finger for the B in bar 3.

Try and hear the tune in your head before playing it. Observe the *tenuto* mark: hold and lean into the last chord.

13 Follow the TRaK

    Can you find all the notes to be sharpened?

    ? What do you notice about the semiquaver figures?

Tap this rhythm a few times:

Play the tonic chord.

Notice how each semiquaver figure consists of broken chord or scale passages.

Play lightly and evenly.

14 **T** Can you count the beats while playing bar 4?

    R Can you tap the rhythm, both parts together?

Give the rests their correct values throughout the piece.

Take care with the rhythm in bar 5:

R.H. [rhythm notation] 1 and 2 and 3   4

L.H. [rhythm notation]

    K What is the key?

Remember **both** sharps in the key signature.

TRaK Is the key major or minor?

Notice the use of C♯. Play the broken chord in bar 1. Now name the key.

Notice how the melody moves into the bass in bar 3 and then returns to the treble again.

? Can you find all the slurred couplets?

Can you study the marked fingering?

Contrast the slurs with crisp *staccato* notes.

Be prepared to place the 3rd finger on the F (RH) in bar 7.

TRaK

Time the group of semiquavers accurately.

In bar 3 see that the right hand enters at the correct time after the **quaver** rest.

This is a short piece but each bar contains something important to be studied before playing. Contrast the slurs in bars 1 and 2 with the *staccato* notes in bar 3. Bar 4 should be very smooth and it begins as quiet as you can manage. However, almost immediately, you need to start a big *crescendo* so that the main theme can return triumphantly in bar 5.

17 | **TRaK**

? Can you find a broken octave?

Can you plan the fingering yourself?

Tap the rhythm in bars 1 and 2 a few times.

Find all the notes to be raised a semitone.

If you have small hands play towards the edge of the notes when stretching an octave.

Practise moving from the interval of a third to the low G minim in the last bar.

Play in a fairly slow and stately manner. As usual, look ahead.

18 | **TRaK**

? What do you notice about the patterns of the notes when you compare bars 1 and 5?

What is the meaning of the sign above and below the minims in bars 2, 4, 6 and 8?

Find all the notes to be lowered a semitone.

Make sure the minims are held for their full value.

This piece is mainly *staccato* and should be played very rhythmically in a marching style.

TRaK

Can you spot the rhythmic pattern on which most of this piece is based?

 Can you work out a fingering for the left hand?

Count and tap the following several times:

Drop the wrist on the first note and lift the wrist on the second when playing the slurred couplets.

 TRaK

 Can you find a tied note?

Do you notice the slurred couplets in bars 1 to 5 (LH)?

Can you study the marked fingering and discover any changes of hand position?

Hold the tie for the correct value. Also be sure to hold the dotted minim in bar 15 for its full length.

Drop the wrist on the first note and then lift it slightly on the second, diminishing the tone on the last note.

Note that in bar 6 (RH) the 2nd finger moves *over* the thumb. In bars 10 and 15 (LH), the thumb should move neatly *under* the 2nd finger.

Before you start, name the key and remind yourself of all the notes to be sharpened.

21 **TRaK**

K In which form of the minor scale does an F♯ appear as well as a G♯?

? What do you notice when you compare bars 1 and 2 with bars 5 and 6?

! **Watch out** for the interval of a second in bar 3 and see that it enters exactly on the second beat.

Find all the accidentals.

The D♯ in bar 4 suggests a change of key. Try to name it.

Notice how the melody is divided between the hands in bar 3.

22 **TRaK**

R Can you tap the rhythms of bars 1 and 5 carefully? Which two bars do **not** include a syncopated rhythm?

? Do you notice the imitation between the first two bars (RH) and bars 3 and 4 (LH)?

! **Watch out** for the interval of a third in bar 6, where the left thumb turns under the 2nd and 3rd fingers.

Common time means that there are …. beats in a bar.

The rest in bar 2 (RH) and in bar 4 (LH) followed by the quaver entry should be exactly timed.

Compare the second half of bar 5 with bar 6 and note the similarities in the melody.

Note the extension between thumb and 2nd finger in the last bar (LH).

TRaK

? How many tied notes are there?

Do you notice the repetition of bars 1 and 2 (RH) in bars 3 and 4 (LH)?

What do you think *energico* means?

Name the accidentals in bars 6, 7 and 8.

Hold all the ties for their full value.

The same rhythm appears in bars 9–11 (LH).

There is no need to play this very fast in order to achieve the right rhythmical style.
Be careful to count four steady beats through bars 7 and 8 since it is all too easy to speed up in these bars.

TRaK

? Are there any tied notes?

Find any accidentals.

Do not confuse a tie with a slur.

Play in a gently flowing motion. Remember all the sharps in the key signature. Look ahead.

TRaK

Look at the time signature; tap the rhythm; and find all the sharps affected by the key signature.

? What are the intervals in the right hand part?

Find the one interval of a second (LH).

Can you try out the suggested fingering for the right hand chords in bars 5 and 7?

In bars 5 and 7 hold the top note of the first chord with the 5th finger while the thumb moves to its next note. This will help you join the two chords smoothly.

Slightly separate the slurred *staccato* notes. Play the coda *pianissimo*. Choose a sensible tempo.

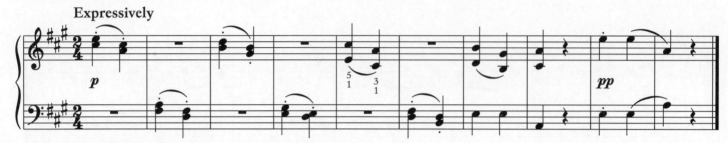

26

TRaK

K Is the key major or minor?

Find all the accidentals.

? What do you notice about the accompaniment? Where does it begin?

Play the chord (RH and LH) which is repeated so frequently.

What do you notice about the melodic intervals in the right hand of bars 3, 4 and 5?

Note the descending sequence in bars 6, 7 and 8.

This piece is more modern and not as difficult as it first appears. Play very slowly and solemnly (*Grave*).

TRaK

Can you find in which bars this rhythm appears?

? Can you practise moving your hand position from bar 1 to bar 3 (RH), and in 7 (LH)?

What is the meaning of *vivace*?

This piece is based mainly on the following rhythmic figure. Tap it a few times:

Prepare the fingers for the broken octaves in bar 5 (LH) and bar 6 (RH).

Observe all the slurs and *staccato* notes.

Aim for a strong contrast in dynamics in bars 6 and 7.

TRaK

Can you tap and count the main rhythmic figure several times?

? Can you name the broken chord in bar 5 (RH)?

Can you suggest a suitable fingering for bars 1 to 3 (RH)?

Give the meaning of **C** in the time signature.

There are many examples of syncopation here. The strong accent, usually found on the first beat of a bar, is displaced to what would normally be a weaker beat.

This is the dominant chord in the key of C.

Take care with the fingering in the small chromatic passage in bar 4.

Play rhythmically. Keep your eyes on the music and always look ahead.

T How many beats are there in a bar?

R Can you count and tap the rhythm in bars 3 and 4?   Time the rests carefully.

K What is the key?   The G♯ and tonic will help you decide on the key.

? What are the intervals in bars 6, 7 and 8 (RH)?   Play these before you begin.

What do you notice when you compare the two phrases?   Notice how the melody is transferred to the left hand in bar 3 for the remainder of the piece.

Think of the rhythm of bar 2 as you play bar 1. Each minim must last for precisely four quavers.

T   A minuet is a graceful dance in …… time.

R Can you tap the rhythm of the first four bars?   Hold the long notes for their full value.

K Is the key major or minor?   Find all the B♭s and accidentals.

? Can you study the fingering?   Note the contractions and extensions in bars 2–3 (RH).

TRaK

Can you tap the rhythm a few times?

Can you find all the F♯s and accidentals?

? What is the meaning of *Allegretto*?

This piece is based mainly on the same rhythmic figure as No. 13:

Although the key is minor, the final chord is major. This effect is called a *tierce de Picardie*.

Look for a *tenuto* mark. Observe the slurred couplets and *staccato* notes.

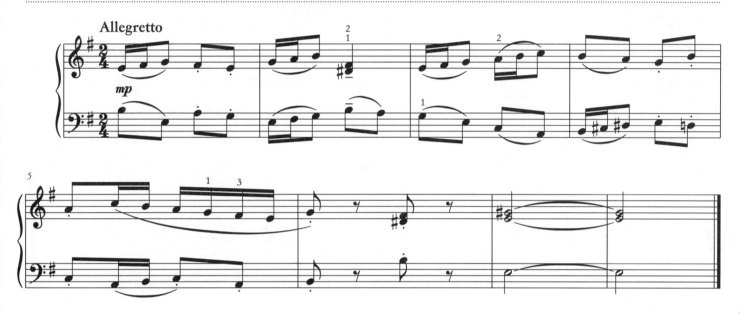

TRaK

What is the value of the beat?

? Why not try out the right hand chord in bar 12 on its own first?

Is there a coda?

This is simple triple time. Try to convey the feeling of one main beat per bar, rather than three quaver beats.

In bars 9, 10 and 11, be sure to hold the dotted crotchets in the right hand for their full value.

Find the bar where the coda begins.

Play all the *staccato* notes crisply, observing the dynamics especially from bar 9 to the end.

33 **TRaK**

? What is the key of this music?   Try to remember all three sharps in the key signature.

Make sure you keep to a really firm pulse and try to 'take in' the music for both hands at the same time, rather than looking at each stave separately. It will help if you can recognise chord shapes, such as the many thirds in this piece, at a *single* glance – however, always try to look at the music, and not your hands, as you play.

34 **TRaK**

Can you tap this rhythm several times, counting four quaver beats?

? What do you notice when you compare bars 1 and 2 with bars 5 and 6?

This piece in simple quadruple time has a quaver beat.

This rhythm may take some practice to get right: try to *feel* the pattern rather than always having to count it.

The contrast between *staccato* and slurred notes is important in this dance style and can be exaggerated.

Notice how the melody is divided between the two hands in bars 2 and 6.

A tango is a dance from Argentina. There is no need to play it too quickly – it can have a feeling of suspense.

Introducing the keys of E, B♭ and E♭ major, and G minor

Can you follow the [TRaK] as usual?

[?] Do you remember the rules regarding accidentals?

Can you find all the tied notes?

Look at the accidentals before naming the key.

Note that some Cs are sharpened, while others are natural. There are B♭s in bars 3 and 9 (LH).

Hold the ties for their correct value and sustain the final chord as you count four full beats.

Try hearing the melody in your head before you play. This is another piece that ends with a *tierce de Picardie*.

[TRaK]

[?] Can you name the interval in bar 6 (LH)?

Do you notice that the melody starts with a a descending sequence?

How many beats should you count for the chord in bar 4?

[!] **Watch out** for the in bar 3 (LH).

Find all the flats.

Play the broken chords in block form.

Note the contrary motion figure in bar 5.

Check for any changes of hand position.

Try to imagine what the melody will sound like before playing it. Remind yourself again of all the flats.

TRaK

Can you spot all the tied notes?
Do you see the descending scales in bars 5–8?

Can you study the fingering, especially bars 6 and 8 (RH) where the 3rd finger turns over the thumb?

Try to remember all four sharps affected by the key signature. There is also an accidental in bar 12 (LH).

Practise the right hand only from bar 11 to the end to get the timing of the ties right.

In bar 6 (LH) note that the thumb turns under the 3rd finger.

Remind yourself again of all the sharps in the key signature. Then play confidently but not too fast.

Smoothly

T

R

K How is this key related to the minor key in No. 35?

Do you notice how the melody gradually ascends?

Give the time signature.

Tap the rhythm of the first two bars (RH) a few times noticing on which beats the two quavers appear.

Find all the notes which have to be lowered a semitone.

Give the meaning of *sempre staccato*.

Play rhythmically and in a lively manner. Try not to look at the keyboard.

Animato

T

R Can you tap the ♩. ♪♪ rhythm a few times?

In what key does the piece begin? (The F♯ is a clue.)

? What does *cantabile* mean?

This is in simple triple time and the beat is a ....

Keep counting.

Notice that the key changes to the relative major for the second half of the piece.

You could try using the pedal for the last two bars.

Try sight-singing the melody line. Then play with a good *legato* tone and make the piece flow.

T

R Can you tap the rhythm of bar 1 a few times?

K What is the key?

? Can you see the sequence in the first two bars (RH)?

Look at the time signature.

The whole piece is based on the figure in this first bar.

In bar 4 the E♮ (RH) suggests a brief change of key to F major, although E♭ is quickly restored by the LH.

Notice that the coda in bar 7 echoes the previous bar.

Contrast the *legato* semiquaver passages with the *staccato* notes.

41 ☐T☐

☐R☐ Can you spot all the tied notes?

☐K☐ Can you find all the notes to be sharpened?

☐?☐ Which finger would you use for the first E in bar 1 (RH)?

Here is another simple triple time signature with a quaver beat.

The quaver rests should be carefully timed.

Also find any accidentals.

Note the slight change of hand position at bar 3 (LH).

Remind yourself again of the sharps in the key signature.
Play fairly slowly with a gentle tone observing the *dim.* and the *rit.* at the end of the piece.
Be very careful to hold the final chord for its full value – listen and count as the sound dies away.

Introducing the keys of B minor and C minor

T How else could this time signature be written?

It is **not** the same as **C**, which has four beats per bar. $\frac{2}{2}$ has only two beats per bar, more like $\frac{2}{4}$ than $\frac{4}{4}$ time.

R What note value is the beat?

When you play the piece, make sure your rhythm sounds as if there are only two main beats per bar.

K What Is the key?

If you are not sure about the key look at the A♯ and the tonic, or key-note, in the bass of the last bar.

! **Watch out** for the E♯ in bar 8 (LH): it is the same note on the piano as F(♮). You may want to try out bars 8–9 before you play the whole piece.

Aim for a dramatic contrast in bars 6–7 and again in bar 8.

TRaK

This piece is in simple triple time. Try to give it the feel of just one beat per bar, not three quaver beats.

K Can you name the key?

The B♮ is a clue, and the piece begins and ends on the tonic note of the key.

? Can you spot the broken chord in bars 1–2?

This broken chord is on the 'tonic triad' of the key.

The first phrase mark crosses the staves, showing that the notes need to flow smoothly from left hand to right hand without any gaps in the sound.

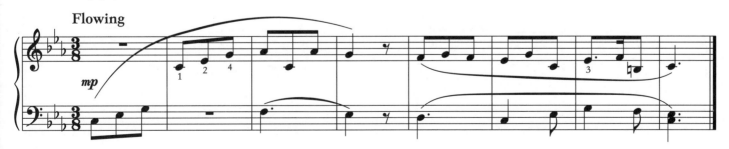

44

T   What does the **8** in the time signature tell you?

This piece is in simple triple time.

R   Can you tap the rhythm, both hands, particularly in bars 3 and 16?

The rhythm in bars 5, 7, 9 and 13 also needs careful timing.

K   Can you name the relative major of C minor?

Find all the flats and naturals.

?   What do you notice when you compare bars 1 and 2 with bars 14 and 15, both hands?

Notice the sequence in bars 5 to 10 (RH).

Play with vigour and a good strong tone. Observe the *staccato* notes. Look ahead and try not to hesitate.

45

T   How else could you write this time signature?

There are two minim beats per bar.

R   Can you imagine a rhythm of eight quavers in bars 2 and 4 as you play the first line of music?

Remember there are 4 quavers to a beat in this time. Be careful not to rush in bars 2 and 4.

K   What is the key?

Notice the A♯ and last note. Now play the tonic chord.

Make sure that all the quaver passages are smooth and secure.
Play this piece fairly quickly, trying to convey a feeling of two minim beats per bar rather than four crotchet beats.

Right@Sight
Right@Sight
Right@Sight
Right@Sight

On your own now ...

The following pieces do not have hints to help.

Remember… follow the TRaK, look ahead, keep counting and keep going!

Moderato

46

March

47

Vivace

48

Allegro

Allegretto

Stately

Ben marcato (march)

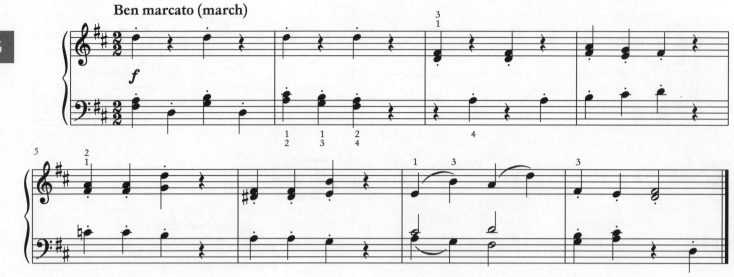

Moderato

Dolce (waltz)

Steady

61

Andante

62

Allegro

63

Semplice

Fast

Andante

Sadly

Waltz

Cantabile

Folk dance (with energy)

Moderato

Stately

Moderato

Fanfare

Cheerfully

Glossary of musical terms and symbols

Adagio	Slowly
Alla breve	[²⁄₂ or ₵] two minim beats in a bar
Alla marcia	In the style of a march
Allegretto	Fairly quick, not as fast as *Allegro*
Allegro	(*lit.* cheerful) Quick, lively
Andante	Walking pace; moderate speed
Animato	Animated
Ben marcato	(*lit.* well) Strongly accented
Cantabile	In a singing style
Coda	(*lit.* a tail) A small passage added to the end of a piece
Con brio	With vigour
Con espressione	With expression
Con moto	With movement
Crescendo, cresc.	Gradually becoming louder
Diminuendo, dim.	Gradually becoming quieter
Dolce	Sweet
Energico	Energetic
*Forte (**mf**, **f**, **ff**)*	Loud (moderately loud, loud, very loud)
Giocoso	Playful, humorous
Grave	Very slow and solemn
Grazioso	Graceful
Legato	Smooth
Leggiero	Light
Lento	Slow
Moderato	Moderate speed
*Piano (**mp**, **p**, **pp**)*	Quiet (fairly quiet, quiet, very quiet)
Più	More
Poco	Little
Rallentando, rall.	Gradually becoming slower
Ritenuto, rit.	Held back
Ritmico	Rhythmically
Semplice	In a simple, unaffected style
Sempre	Always
Spiritoso	In a spirited manner
Staccato	Detached
Tempo di menuetto	In the time (and style) of a minuet
Tempo giusto	In strict time
Tenuto	Held (𝆮 ♩)
Tierce de Picardie	(*Fr.* for Picardy third)
	A *major* tonic chord which concludes a piece in a minor key
Vivace	Lively, quick
𝄐 *(Fermata)*	Pause
>	Accent